THIS IS IT

WHEN DESIRES BECOME GOD'S ANSWERS

Heather White-Davis

Copyright © 2025 by Heather White-Davis

All rights reserved. No part of this book may be used or reproduced in any form whatsoever without written permission except in the case of brief quotations in critical articles or reviews.

Printed in the United States of America or Canada

For more information or to book an event, contact :
info@cojbookz for publishing
For public speaking by Heather White Davis
booksbypastorheather@yahoo.com
WhatsApp Phone Number 1-646-463-2721

ISBN - Paperback: 978-1-998120-86-4

DEDICATION

I want to dedicate this book to of course my Heavenly Father and the Holy Spirit that inspired me to write even when I felt so depressed and overwhelmed in that season but I want to also dedicate this book to some key persons that inspired and motivated me to continue the journey when I felt like it didn't make sense and life wasn't fair at all. Mr. Michael Uter, who has been one of the key factors in the season of my life when I really needed that individual father figure and friend to just be there. There were some days when my faith was tested, and I began to just complain that I can't be bothered, but he encouraged me with his firm words of affirmation and love that this is it, and this too shall pass. I know that God is the author and the finisher of my story, but even the people that He chooses to represent Him in our seasons are so important and relevant, and so I dedicate this book to you, my friend. I also want to dedicate this book to my spiritual mother Apostle Martha Spencer who in this season, you were the shoulder and the ears that I could depend on. The many nights when I couldn't sleep, and your number was the only one I wanted to call because I knew you would pray for me. You cried with me, you told me that things are going to work out for the good soon, you counseled me with words of wisdom and you expressed a mother's love to me even when you lost your husband you were still being that mother to me To every woman and men that have gone through seasons of trauma or lost or you might be trapped in a place and can't find your way out or just need that word of advice, to the ones like myself who have reached this cross road and have said This is it, I dedicate this book to you.

INTRODUCTION

August 17, 2024, 6:37 am
Saturday morning

As I lay here in bed with thoughts of what the day will bring, as today is my Reshuffle Outreach Ministry Youth Conference and Pre-Birthday Celebration and my thoughts should be one of anticipation of excitement right but it's the other way around.
You see, so much has been happening especially over the last six months, and I have been so suppressed and being depressed while trying to balance Ministry and my personal life the best way I possibly can, especially in the eyes of the public. Deep within I was collapsing and trying to make the right decisions, trying to hear what God is saying and what others were saying plus what my spirit was saying was so much of a battle. I had to be fighting these past six months and of course there were persons who I had confided in that I would call for Godly advice and counseling and I would somewhat feel at ease but then the situations would like a sudden earthquake, just happen.
At times I would sense that yes this is coming but then unaware they would just present themselves and these were the most dramatic and overwhelming and stressful periods I would undergo, so here I am this morning saying Lord I thank you for today, thank you for waking me up this morning and then my thoughts just begins to run wild, I call them Reshuffled thoughts.

The things that had occurred over the last 4 weeks began to replay in my head, and I began to surf my way through. My mind begins to tick like a clock, and for every tick it's a thought: What should I do? And of course, no answer because the tick welcomes the tock, so no space for an answer, then I'm left with just my 4 favorite words; Lord speak to me. I said, "Lord, I know you have spoken to me before, and I know your voice. You have sent messages through your servants repeatedly, but this morning, I am like Gideon. Let somebody that I don't know, one that is not aware of what's happening, give me a word that's coming directly from you. I need to hear you again for clarity this morning."

Then, as I steered into the ceiling of my bedroom, I heard, "This is it. When desires become God's answer," I was like, ok God, but this sounds like a book, and I heard begin to write and hence I turned over took up my phone, and I began to write.

CHAPTER 1

THERE'S A WAR IN THE MIND

I don't believe that mentally and maybe emotionally, I was all that stable in my thinking, and not to mention physically. Over the past 3 weeks, I have been fighting to stay physically, spiritually, mentally, and also emotionally strong. The doctor requested that I do some blood works and a mammogram after doing his inspections at my last visit and by the following day I had to rush back to the Doctor's office because of one of those earthquake sudden experiences that visited me that morning and woke me out of my sleep that gave me a splitting headache leaving the left side of my face with a dancing sensation.
The Doctor advised me that my blood pressure was low from the day before, so now this had put me in what's called a stroke trigger, He said to me. "What is happening"? I took a deep sigh, then briefly related a summary, and he responded, saying. "Whoever it is that's causing these reactions doesn't matter who, Block them or turn off your phone because your mental health is more important."
With advice like this from your Doctor, means this thing is really serious right? When the person who's behind this is not a stranger, especially if the person is your significant other, children, family members who are very close or even your Boss/Supervisor at work, etc., now this is where it gets even more complicated. Let's say my husband, in this case, or my child, how can I block or turn off my phone or not talk to them? But the reality is your mental health supersedes

whoever is the main cause of your triggers, hence it comes down to a radical decision that only you must make.

Sometimes we're forced to make decisions that are very difficult but healthy, and I had to do the right thing. Sometimes the enemy will let you to believe that doing right is wrong, and at times the best decisions will leave you feeling uncomfortable, even feeling like you're being selfish. This is what the devil does to us. He plays on our emotions, leaving us to believe we're monsters and we have no compassion, especially if you're a Christian. He reminds us of scriptures that speaks of love and compassion, but this is just a scheme of manipulation.

God is love, that's the first thing we need to remember so if whosoever it is or was that caused you to be in a situation that compromised your health and well being, is not operating in the love of God but rather obsessions and selfishness. When you love someone, you have total respect for that person.

You express your love in a manner to give not to take. You give your kind words and affirmations, not tear down and slander. You give your affection, showing them they're secure around you, not fear and terror. When you love someone, you rebuke in love, not in embarrassment, to cause trauma or low self-esteem, but for self-inspection where an apology is necessary.

Oftentimes, we are so accustomed to abuse and trauma that even when we are Christians, we accept it and become psychologically vulnerable, but *This Is It!* We must take a stance by making the choice to close any doors in our lives that were opened for mental illness.

Some days were good, very good too, sometimes melancholy was the feeling I had to deal with, and in the midst of all this, there were persons I had to be counseling and interceding for. I had to preach to God's people, greet with a beautiful smile but going home messed up in my mind, which would often leave me emotional with tears are just lost in a battlefield in my mind.

The mind is the center of the battlefield; that's the place the devil takes pleasure in visiting most. He knows that, that's where God releases His word that gives us hope and peace to comfort our hearts, and that's why the Bible instructs us in Ephesians 6:10-19 to put on the whole Armor of God.

Without having on the full Armor of God, we are firstly not strong and secondly we cannot defeat the enemy. The warfares of the mind is not a physical one that we are able to see with our physical eyes, they are not carnal but spiritual and if the enemy can win the battles of our minds that's it, we're totally defeated and that's why the Apostle Paul encourages us In Phillipians 4:8 that there must be a finally based on what we allow our minds to think on. It's not always easy to navigate through our thoughts because the battles are oftentimes so intense especially when the enemy knows there's a breakthrough just ahead, he will stop at nothing but to defeat the plans and purposes of God for our lives but God's word is already spoken and if we can just think on it for a second then we can gain strength to defeat the enemy for we can do all things through Christ who strengthens us (Phillipians 4:13)

Strength is what every believer needs to overcome the battles of the mind. Let us bear in mind that with a weak mindset, we will only produce failure. Failure in our spirituality by not being able to read the Word of God, prayerlessness becomes a strong hold, lack of strength to praise and worship, everything we look at begins with an attempt of fear, doubt prevents us from moving forward, we no longer trust what we know to be truth and we become a defeated foe but when we can push our selves to believe on what the Word of God says and make a cry for help that's when the spirit of God will pull us to a place where every mind binding spirits that held us captive must now break and let us loose to gain strength to now call on our helper the Holy Spirit.

This is how the mind will begin to think on things that reflects on what the God in us says we know that all things work together for good for them that love God and are called according to His Word.
I am now at a place in my life where I have decided not to allow my mind to activate weakness because this is the place of defeat and strength. I have cultivated a practice where, as soon as I begin to think on the negative, I begin to speak to myself and encourage myself with the word of God. I remind myself first that my life is not my own and that I belong to Jesus Christ. I begin to declare who I am and what I believe. What do you believe about yourself today? At the end of this chapter, there are blank pages that you now need to write with all honesty.

Can you take a moment and begin to ask yourself these simple questions: Who am I? What is my purpose? Why am I at this place physically, mentally or emotionally? Am I who God says I am, and do I believe? When you begin to write your truth, you are letting go of built-up emotions that had you lying to yourself, and this is where you will be broken for deliverance to happen. Deliverance
from the past or present strongholds of the mind and giving yourself the best gift ever. Mental Freedom. Now this is a

decision you may or may not choose to take, but it's up to you to believe.

Believing God's word is paramount important to be strong in our decisions. You can choose to believe you can't or can, but it depends on how much you know God's word. It is God's word that I know and trust that caused me to believe that I would no longer be defeated. It is God's word that caused me to take a stance to come out of the bed of adultery. It is God's word that caused me to begin to believe in myself, that there's much more to life than being a failure.
It is God's word that I believed and spoke it into existence that I am a conqueror through Christ Jesus. I declared God's word and believed it that I will not die when I felt insanity knocking at my mind's door as if to tear it down to enter. I declared His word with confidence that my mind is the mind of Christ and that I will not fear no evil.

Deliverance comes when you believe God's word over your circumstances. The enemy will always wage war against the believer, but he can only win when you decide not to believe in the word of God over your life. What are you believing over your life now? The situation might be a just cause for you not to believe but what does the word of God say?

The enemy knows when we are most vulnerable, this is his best strategy of attack. Job said the thing I greatly feared the most has come upon me, and the thing I was afraid of has come unto me. Job 3:25.
What do you fear greatly right now? What is it that you are afraid of? As you pause to ask yourself this question, can you honestly answer? You see, God loves it when we are honest first with ourselves, then with Him. It's all about the battlefield of the mind because if the enemy can keep us through our thoughts to be fearful and afraid, then he has

defeated us, but when we can be honest with ourselves and with God, then that's how the Holy Spirit will be able to deliver us. Remember, He is the Spirit of truth, and the spirit of lies will continue to war against the Spirit of truth but until we come to finally to allow truth to fight, then we will be defeated.

Satan already knows that every believer as a weakness even when we pray and believe that we are so strong that we can do the thing we believe we're equipped to handle and that's why it is the mind that he targets because if he can just touch that area that we still struggle with, he will get to our heart and that's where all the issues of life flows.
Proverbs 4:23. It's a battle to guard our hearts if our minds are not guarded. Imagine the enemy comes to us after everything around us, like Job, is taken away just like that, and he comes in the form of a loved one as Job's wife, telling us curse God and die.

If our minds are not affixed with the helmet of salvation to plead the blood of Jesus Christ against the deception immediately then what will happen is our heart will begin to weigh the word that was released and right there and then the enemy attack our vulnerability and we find ourselves faced with the consequences of depression, suppression and even suicidal thoughts and we begin to look at God as a wicked God when it's a warfare we're now faced with. We will then begin to lose hope, trust and faith in God so we're no longer able to stand as victors in spite of what is happening, but we are now victims of the enemies plots against us. And that's why it is so important that we study the Word of God and meditate on it.
Believers, we have to understand that God will not go back on His word. The Bible says in Matthew 5:18 before one jot of His word passes, heaven and earth will pass, Psalm 138:2 says

God honors His word above His name. What am I saying, when our hearts desires comes up before God, He will respond to you in your favor, for God will grant us the desires of our hearts, Psalm 37:4 but until we come to the place of truth where we're convicted to repent and ask God's forgiveness and boldly declare that This is it! No more will I be bound by my desires, no more will I be held captive by my foolish decisions and prideful choices, no longer will I allow my mind to entertain the lies and manipulations of the enemies tricks but I will take a stance to finally release my mind to think and believe on the Word of God over my life.

Notes

CHAPTER 2
HOW TO TRANSITION

When I came to grips or better yet, the reality of the truth with myself and began to examine myself. I had to encourage myself and evaluate who I am, knowing who God has called me to become and that the picture was not in alignment of what God had shown me. I had to make a crucial decision to either remain in stagnation or step out in boldness and become the replica of the Christ that lives and resides in me. Now transitioning is never easy. First, you will be forced to deal with the manipulative thoughts from the enemy that will speak through your mind.

There will be the attacks of guilt asking why, Are you sure, what if you're wrong, what will others think or say and the questions will keep coming, putting you at a place of uncertainty and if not careful depression enters and this will keep you indecisive with not knowing what to do and how to do it but again this is where you have to rely on the word of God to help you.

Psalm 34:6 Sometimes all it takes is a cry for help. It's ok to cry and cry all you can but let not your cry be of sympathy but of help. I remember when I was at the place of transitioning, I was so confused because of the many questions I was faced with and none of these questions were about my well being but of other's reactions towards my decisions and I was struggling with depression until I broke down before the Lord and I said God, I need your help.

I was truthful to my Father. I said God, I have failed you again and I'm sorry, please help me to rise beyond my defeat, help me to walk righteous before you again, help me to live Holy, as

this is your desire for me, pull me out of this mess I put myself in and rewrite my story Lord.
Help me Father because I am weak, I can't stand unless you lift me up, I can't walk into your will except your will be done in me, God I surrender my life over to you and deliver me from the hands of the enemy and use me as your mouthpiece to declare your testimony for others to be delivered. If you can pray this same prayer that I prayed, I am sure that the same deliverance I received then, you too will also receive the same. In Jesus name, Amen.

God delivered me that night. I remembered that after crying out to God for help I heard the Spirit of God instructing me what to do and how to do it. The Bible says in 1 Corinthians 1:27 that He uses the foolish and the base things of this world to confound the wise. The instructions seemed foolish but I didn't take thought because I knew the voice of God, and I did everything how I was being instructed and can I tell you I came forth delivered and free to make the next step into my transition.

You also have to understand that when God speaks, it is so. I wondered how would I transmit the messages He had given me to those whom I had to cut and sever contacts with but I heard Him say softly "I will do that" and it came with such peace. I didn't have to tell any lies or make any excuses, God just did it, hallelujah. I could speak with boldness and confidence, I wasn't afraid to say No or yes without thinking of how the person or persons would feel why I had been delivered so the transition came easy.

> Now there's another phase in the transition that's not a walk in the park, and it's the phase where the opposition will put up a defense. The opposer is used to being in control and so it won't be an easy step for them to let go. They will fight to

hold on and they will give you reasons why you shouldn't let go and reason why you should re-think your decision but again when you have a relationship with God and when you allow God's word to take preeminence in your life, you will stand your ground even when you feel like you're being too hard.

The opposer will play the victim and will also lure others to join them in opposing your decision. In most cases the opposer will build an army to try and attack your integrity and your character but do not be distracted. Remember all the enemy wants is to get to your mind again to start another battle but safeguard your mind,
and your heart will also be guarded. This is where you speak less and pray more. Cut communications as best as possible and avoid direct contact, whether through in person or telephone calls or messages. Stand on what you said and do not fold when it becomes overwhelming because it will. Get involved into prayer sessions and worship is the main strategy you need to implement. If you can change your geographical location, that's a plus, but if not, ask the Lord to make a shift where you can take a vacation from work and home just to get out of the sphere you're accustomed to and where your opposer is looking to find you.
When your mind is renewed, it's the most beautiful gift you could give yourself. Your strength will also be renewed and restored and you will begin to walk into your purpose, knowing who you are and what it is that God wants you to become.

Sometimes people believe that losing those who once meant the world to them is a bad thing — especially based on the lies the enemy has fed to the majority but in order to transition perfectly you must cut ties with some contacts and sometimes this is painful but you will soon realize that you should have done this sooner than you did.

You see, God is not the author of confusion and He will not allow you whom He has chosen and called out of darkness, to still operate in darknes,s meaning living in sin. Know when it's time to transition from one season to the next. Many of us miss our seasons because of fear of letting go, fear of starting over, fear of what others will say or think and sometimes fear of not knowing where you're going but Abraham wasn't told where he was going but he was told to leave his father's house, kindred and country, Genesis 12:1-3.

Transition is not always a walk in the park but if you can listen to the voice of God even when it doesn't seem to make any sense whatsoever but I promise you that like Abraham, your obedience will reward you with great blessings. Oftentimes, we waste years in setbacks because we feared to transition. If God is speaking to you today that it's your season to transition, don't be stiff-necked and stubborn. Save your generation.

Be the vessel that God had carved you into being. Stop merely existing and understand that true existence is in living an obedient life through God's Word for your life. You were not created to please man but to please God. Our lives should not just reflect what our abilities can do but the ability to do what God has called us to be through Him.

Transitioning is not just a physical one but a spiritual one where others will no longer look at you for you but they will see the Christ that resides in you and this will cause them to want to receive Him and walk into this transition and glorify Him that lives in you. Matthew 5:16.

Begin to write:

What is it that is holding me back from fulfilling my God's given purpose in the earth?

Am I just living or existing into a place of dormancy or growth?

What do I want for Me?

Am I a reflection of God's image and likeness?

Is there more in me than I truly believe?

Can I really become that which I would like to?

How can I do this?

When you write these questions, think about them, then answer truthfully. The Word of God is the inspiration of truth and life. When you release His Word over your mind, your body comes into alignment, and the Holy Spirit responds with Revelations. It's your time to transition to the next level of where and what God intends for your life.

<u>Notes</u>

CHAPTER 3
DON'T CRITICIZE WHAT YOU DON'T UNDERSTAND

People will judge and criticize you not always based on what they know which is the truth or facts, but more often, you will be judged and criticized based on what they either heard or what looked like. Now, when your desires become God's answer, things will appear to be true and oftentimes we're living in so much misery and disappointment and discomfort because of what our hearts desired. Can you attest to this? Well I am glad that God would have chosen me to write this book so that you who is reading will understand that whether you want to admit it or not you're not alone.

You see, throughout my life in sin and in grace I have allowed the desires of my heart to gain me God's answer and I was at first so happy, believing, yes thank you Jesus you came through for me, this is it. God shows us enough signs not to but our hearts desires are always fixed on what we believe is right for us and God will not put up any resistance with us; instead, He will gladly release to us what our hearts desires.

I want us to understand that God is not just a God who will choose for us no, He allows us through our soul, where our emotions are, to make our own choices. God will show us the right but allows us to make the choice to do good or bad. He's a loving Dad but also a wise Father so if you won't listen then you will somehow hear or feel but He will always be there when disappointment or destruction comes knocking us down and like any child that runs back to their parents, will have to run back to Him when we finally realize that He was right all this time.

I have made some huge mistakes because of what my heart desired. The most crucial ones were my failed marriages. I did not listen to the voice of God but my own self will. As a Christian and especially when you're supposed to be at a place of maturity in God where you know Him, you have a relationship with Him, you're not expected to fall into mistakes or failures and this is the biggest mistake we all make as leaders. Not because we might be more mature or advanced than others in knowing the Word doesn't mean that we're not prone to mistakes or failures.

And that's why we must be careful of the spirit called self and pride.
God specifically inspired normal men who had gone through the same test we have or might be going through to write books so that we could read and recognize that we're just human but that what they went through is now for an example for us to learn but we oftentimes tend to take away the Evangelism messages to preach salvation which is very good but we leave out the message of character building and we fall into the same sins as they did. We need to be reminded that God is a dependable and Intentional God, hence He expects us to depend on Him in order to live this Holy and Righteous lifestyle through Him and not what we believe we can through maturity in believing we know the Word.
The devil is also mature and he knows the Word and as a matter of fact, he's even more advanced in maturity and in knowledge of the Word than any of us as Pastors or Christians could ever be and that's why we have to depend on God all the time.

Moses is an ideal character reference we can use. God spoke face to face with Moses. God used Him to deliver His people from Egypt, working signs and wonders. God used Moses to do great exploit on His behalf but Moses had an issue for he had the spirit of Anger so he strike the rock not as how God instructed him but how his heart felt towards the people who were constantly sinning against God but even though Moses's intentions were in defense of God he was in breach of God's instructions and oftentimes we're caught in the same situation and does it mean that even when God punishes us for our actions He's not with us, or He doesn't loves us? Of course not.

His word says in Hebrews 13:5-6 that He will never leave us nor forsake us so when the enemy don't understand what God is doing then he will always criticize and judge us and sometimes slander us based on our mistakes or falling short situations but the Bible says in Jude 9 that even when Satan came to dispute with Michael the ArcAngel concerning Moses body he could not win. God's Mercies will keep us when we belong to Him, even when it appears like we failed the assignment.

David is another character we should learn from. We know the story of David and his servant Uriah. David's heart desires for Uriah's wife caused him to murder a good servant and he thought he had victory after marrying and impregnating her but the child died because again God will always grant us our hearts desires even when it's not right but for us to learn not to lean to our own self will but to trust God at all times for directions for our lives Proverbs 3:5-6

God sent the prophet in 2 Samuel 11-12, warning David that the sword wouldn't leave his house as a punishment for the wicked act he had done. God said if David desired another wife, He would have granted him and that's how much God loves us. David had many wives and concubines but God was willing to give him another wife according to his heart's desire but what I love about God is that even when he punishes us for our trespasses, He will not leave us or forsake us. When we come before God, acknowledging that we have trespassed against Him from a true place, He will forgive us.

David was broken in the spirit and his heart was contrite before God Psalm 51. He repented of his sins and God forgave him and called him a man after His own heart.

Is your heart after God? Or are you still compromising the Word of God upon your life by engaging in sinfulness? Are you setting your heart on the things of this world or on the things that pleases God? If your answer is yes, I suggest you pause right here and declare Psalms 51 and ask God to deliver your heart now.
When people don't understand your victory over your battles of sin, they are going to speculate, judge and criticize your walk, especially if you're like me and even David, who is expressive in how we worship and praise God. The Bible says in 2 Samuel 6:14-22 that after David had lead the army of Israel into victory against the enemy that he danced in victory before the people and before God that even his clothes fell off.

When God delivers your soul from hell and out of the hands of the enemy, you will not withhold yourself in praise and worship to Him. You will not reserve how you thank Him, you will not think about who is around to give God honor and glory, you will be transparent when you're giving God all that belongs to Him even giving of yourself totally without shame or remorse and many people will not understand your stance but I want to encourage you that if you're like

David's wife Michal who laughed at David and criticized and judged him when he danced to His God until his clothes fell off, I suggest you begin to repent. The Bible said that because she laughed and criticized David, her womb was cursed. Let's not criticize or judge God's servants when we don't fully understand; let's pray for them. Lift them before God in prayer and ask God to restore them and for His will to be done in their seasons.

Pray this prayer with me:

Heavenly Father my Lord and my God. I repent even now Lord for every judgement I released against your servants, unknowingly and knowingly. Forgive me, Lord for participating in conversations about your servants based on something I heard but didn't have full knowledge of. Forgive those who are also partakers and tail bearers and slanderers of your servants, Lord. Father, help me not to be quick to judge and quick to speak but help me to be humble in listening and refrain my lips from speaking guile against your servants.

Father, I pray for restoration over your servants in whatever way they fall short and deliver them from out of the hands of the enemy Lord God. I pray your peace to locate them even now and that you will be glorified through the words of their testimonies in Jesus name. Amen

If you prayed this prayer from a true place, then go ahead and praise God that you have been forgiven and you're free to love upon everyone you have freely forgiven. Hallelujah! Remember, somethings will not appear to be God and sometimes somethings will look good but it's not of God, so before speculating ask God to deal with the situation. It's always better to be in right standing with God than to be against Him.

Never criticize or judge what you don't understand.

CHAPTER 4
RECLAIM AND REDISCOVERING YOU

Now this is another really hard one. The word Reclaim is literally saying taking back what was taken from you and Rediscovering is simply finding back the person who you originally were. Sighhh. I took a long sigh for this one. Now, a lot of people might believe that overtime you're supposed to get it meaning experience teaches wisdom, and that's true but the human nature is so fragile and sometimes so complicated to even comprehend. Mistakes that you made should never happen again, right? But the truth is they do happen again and sometimes again but there must come a time when you will get it and this is where you say: **This Is It.**

I have given myself into submission based on what the Word of God says, Ephesians 5:22, and it's so funny how this scripture is used so often, especially in marital relationships but the question I will pose is this: What is the wife submitting to? The love. According to v/s 25 where the husband was told to love the wife as Christ loves the church right, then can the wife submit if this Christ like love is not being initiated?

I have realized that we tend to absorb our emotions and expels how we feel based on a scripture or two but never the whole chapter or context of the subject at hand. Let's look at what v/s 33 says: Husbands were told to love their wives with humility and sacrifice. Now like myself and many other wives who have encountered a series of abuse, how can we submit when there's no Christ like love given?

I had to teach myself self love because I was so damaged. Growing up with my grandmother and aunts was good but not good enough. The development of a child is well done with both parents input in the child's development and future.

We can always be single parents and do our best in raising our child/ren well and they become successful in education and careers and become financially stable but there's always a void in that child's life when one parent is missing, not to mention both parents.

So I loved my grandmother so much, God bless her soul as she rests in peace but I was so troubled on the inside. The love I desired from my mom and dad was a wish that never came true for me, and I seek for that love in others by trying to do the right things to seek validation that you're worth loving.

As a child, I would wonder why couldn't I be hugged and told I love you by those around me who claimed they love me to others but never expressed it to me.
I would find myself talking to the trees, the dog, my makeshift dolls because I didn't actually ever gotten a real one. Then I would believe that my parents and grandparents never really loved me as they claimed.

The foundation of love first begins with the parents. Now if the parents have never received love, how could they give it? This is deep and this was what I cultivated in my teenage years as a mother that I would love and protect my child or children even if it meant doing it all by myself.

What I didn't receive in the form of love from my parents and family members, I vowed to give to my children even if I had to deprive myself of things to make their lives better than mine. I was willing to make the sacrifice. Love is a sacrifice and that's why Jesus gave His life for us. Can you love someone sacrificially enough to reclaim and rediscover loving yourself the way you should?

When I decided to get married the first time. I was so in love with my first husband that even though he had displayed unfaithfulness and dishonesty, I was willing to sacrifice my love and to submit to what felt like love. Am I the only person who made these regrettable choices? You believe that after divorce, you are now experienced based on what you've been through and now prepared to advance to submit to loving again because you now are
1. Experienced
2. Mature
3. Healed, but are you really and truly?

So after 8 years being single and promiscuous, I thought I was ready to sacrifice and submit again to another man, especially since I have now given my life over to God, but this is always where our biggest mistakes are made.

Given our lives fully to God is the first sacrifice but submitting totally to His will has always been the issue where a lot of us fell short. Submitting totally to God means that every plan, idea, or thought that our soul produces should be entirely submitted to Him. Now this is where the enemy intervenes and most or oftentimes we fail. Why, the process of waiting sometimes is a lengthy one that requires patience, trust and faith in God. This is what sacrifice and submission are. Now, if we have not yet fully mastered the heart of total submission and sacrifice to God first, then it's impossible to do it to man.

I have failed this test when the waiting period came. I thought I had mastered it but let's understand that the waiting period is the testing period, and of cours,e the enemy will come as he did to Job and of course, God will grant him permission to gain access with conditions applied, but this is all to prove that we are now ready to take on the assignment with man.

You cannot take on an assignment if you're not totally in alignment with God's will and purposes for your life.

What is God's will concerning your life and purpose?
Have you enquired of Him what is the next step?

Are you in total surrendering and obedience to God that if the enemy should take something from you at a point where you should be receiving but God says it's ok, are you totally at that place to hear and to stand still and wait?

Some of my mistakes, especially in marriage was disobedience. God spoke. I heard but didn't stand still and wait long enough to see that the enemy also heard and was on assignment, and God will allow him to afflict us because we must get to the place of total submission and sacrifice in Him and to Him.

What I love about God is that He's the greatest Teacher. You see the Holy Spirit is a gentle person and He will never intervene when your hearts desires overrides His instructions, however what He does is He allows us to enter into whatever relationship we choose knowing what the outcome will be but He's waiting patiently to comfort our hearts when they are broken to restore, reset, restart and to reclaim whatever the enemy destroyed.

There will be sometimes when we cannot pray but then that's when He comes and intercedes for us. We were never left alone but were allowed to choose and that's where in choosing, we must totally depend on Him to help us, or we will keep making the same mistakes repeatedly. (Proverbs 3:5-6)

I came to realize that making the choice to submit and to make sacrifices to a man could only happen when I totally commit my entire being, which is my will and emotions to God.

I'm now at a place where I can now reclaim what's mine because I'm now paying attention. I have become like Gideon, Lord I hear you but please give me more confirmations that this is you. I'm not anxious anymore because I have submitted my emotions and I have reclaimed my self worth and my place in God.

Reclaim your minds, Reclaim your heart, Reclaim your soul from that dead place, Reclaim your joy, Stand Up with boldness and confidence knowing your desires are not over ruling God's will for your life and wait for the Spirit of God to lead and direct you into all truth and let your request be made known to Him and watch Him bring your purposes into reality.

CHAPTER 5
DO MORE THAN JUST EXIST

Before the fall of Adam and Eve (who were first made spirit beings, but through sin, they became limited to existing eternal lives), we were created to not just last but to outlast. The enemy who from the beginning deceived and manipulated our core being of existence, and by this deception, we oftentimes operate from a place of limitation when in fact we have the ability to do more. This is why the mind has remained the place where the enemy targets. If the enemy can speak just one word into your mind and you then believe and convey this Word into existence then you will operate from a posture of limitation but if you can realize and understand that what the enemy is saying is contrary to what the Word of God says then you can believe and convey this Word into existence also and operate from a posture of being limitless and this is all in our DNA as humans.

The minute we begin to take thought of what the enemy says, believe and speak it, that's the only access He needs to keep us limited. The Word of God tells us that (Jeremiah 29:11) God knows the plans He has for us, and these plans are all of good and not bad. Before God created us, like our forefather Adam, He knew what He was creating and the purpose of our existence. Can you believe God that, even though we might fall out of alignment of His plans, He's still faithful to His Word towards us and that He can and will realign us back into His will if we allow Him to?

As you reflect on your answer, which I hope that should be a yes, let me ask you another question.

Have you ever thought of doing something or making a life changing decision but then something keeps telling you that you can't do it or it's not possible?

Well, I know that some of you may say no, while some of you, your answer will be yes, and the reason I know that some of you will say yes is, I have also been at this place as a Christian, where I should have all the faith and belief in what God can do again. All the enemy wants is just to get your attention with one word of lie or deception and the minute you take thought of it that's it, so yes He knows how to get the best of us like Judas, David, Peter and much more but even when the enemy succeeds in his attempts, because we were before conception, we were created to outlast, then that's when God will step right in and what the enemy meant for evil, God will turn things around for our good.

I could have been far more advanced than this but because of doubt and fear of what the enemy whispered, I paused or I ran ahead of time. The enemy's intentions are never of good but that of evil. He knew from day one that Adam and Eve were made to outlast and to do more than to just exist.
Genesis 1:22-31 God gave the greatest power and dominance to Adam and Eve, where they had the power and ability to procreate and not just them, but to every living creature on the face of the earth and Man was in total authority of the Earth. So many times, because we do not know the power and the authority that we possess, the enemy comes and deceives us into doing no more than just existing. The enemy understands that if he can keep us in a place of being manipulated, then we would not function according to God's plan. The enemy

understands that He lost His authority, which gave him the ability to do more and so he will continue to fight us from staying in our rightful place and position to be who and what we were created to be.

I want us to always remember that the enemy has great power but He's not all powerful not only that what we have is what He lost and that's authority so if He can work aggressively and assiduously against our minds then He will have not just power over us but He can take full control and that of itself is having authority over us but God is an intentional God and because He knows we are prone to weaknesses He has assigned Angels to encamp in and around us to catch us in case we dash our foot against a stone. (Psalm 91:11-12)

There's so much more to this life that God has allotted to us than merely existing. Existing can put us at a place of limitation, even limiting the plans that God has concerning our future. I remember when I had my first and second child as a teenager. My belief was to just live a failed life and accept whatever was said about me by anyone.
 I literately accepted that I was a failure and began seeing myself at one stage in life a teenage drop out mother with no subjects, living in a society that accepted the practice of under aged girls becoming early mothers who were most often abused by baby fathers who they themselves had accepted society's way of living being a gangster or a street side hang out or an hustler who when the pressures of life hits really hard, leaving them helpless and hopeless. This would now lead them to abuse their children's mothers, which sometimes leads to death and the only reasonable cause was because somebody didn't understand that their position and purpose in life was not

just to exist but to take responsibility for one's mistakes and become who God created man to be, to outlast.

You see, the Bible clearly tells us in Ecclesiastes 3 that to every thing under the sun, there's a time and season but also a purpose to it. What was Soloman saying to us? Things will happen in this life, sometimes things beyond our control, sometimes things we choose or others choose for us and sometimes God Himself allows and ordained before the conception of our being, but whatever it is that our seasons comes with, there's a purpose to it. When we understand this concept of life, we can do more than just existing but being practical, looking forward to outlasting the difficult seasons when they arrive.

I have now grasp this concept and I have moved from just limiting myself from living a good life even when the seasons or trials come. I have learned that seasons don't last and also that time waits on no one to adjust but that there's a purpose to my season and I have to study the seasons based on prior experiences and by seeking the heart of God that He has for me to come out of the season, not as a victim but that of a victor.

There has been so many missed opportunities because I was just existing throughout my seasons. I now understand that I was never made to last the test of times and seasons but to outlast everyone as they came and sometimes they came repeatedly, especially if I failed but I thank God for every failed season as they became my foundatio,n to which today I have built courage and determination to not just last but to outlast.

I know there were some seasons that you too were really just existing and just lasting while they lasted and maybe you are like who I now am a learning vessel that continues to learn by outlasting, while you might be like who I have become, growing and becoming the product of the purpose, You will realize that the season couldn't eliminate you because you out lasted it and this is such a joy to become who God has created us to be.

I am grateful for every lesson I have learned throughout my failed seasons, and I am willing to help someone who's just going through their test to help them to understand that even these seasons were necessary for where God wants to take them.

I am more bolder and confident in the woman I am today, even when others don't see me as the product of change. I am an Overcomer through Christ Jesus, so I just smile at their beliefs, knowing that for this cause I outlasted their opinions of me. Today I can smile not because everything is great but because I am totally happy with myself, that my purpose will come to manifestation because I am purposed to become who God created me to be.

I have many regrets about the choices that I ignorantly and disobediently made ,I am so grateful that I didn't choose to last through them but gave myself the opportunity to outlast my tenure by coming out of them. There's nothing impossible that you can't do when you believe you can do it. The Bible reminds us that we can do all things through Christ, who strengthens us.
Are you allowing Jesus Christ to strengthen you as you go through your season?

I pray that if you're not letting Him do so, will you begin to ask Him to strengthen you right now? Let me pray for you:

> My Father who art in heaven. Today as I approach your throne of grace and mercy on the behalf of my friend, brother, or sister, I stand before you with a repentant heart seeking your forgiveness for every trespass we have trespassed against you and I thank you, Father that you have forgiven us. Lord you have been more than good to us even when we have not been good to you. My Lord there's nothing we have done that you're not aware of and so we come naked before you, surrendering all to you. My Lord as you have lead me through the valley of the shadow of death, I pray that you will also lead these your children, too.
> Remind them not to fear no evil for you are always with us to guard and protect us. My Father as you have taken me out of every failed season into a season of breakthrough, I ask Lord that you take these your children out of there's too into their season of breakthrough. Lord I thank you and I glorify you and I bless you on the behalf of your people in Jesus name Amen.

Shout an hallelujah, shout another hallelujah! Glory to God. I am sure that God has heard this prayer and He will answer you just as He answered me remember to trust the process and don't rush it. God will bring you through.

Can you take a moment and begin to reflect on your season, begin to write what you have been going through.

Write what you're believing God to do for you and give Him time to work with you.

Write Him a promissory note on what you will be doing for Him when He takes you out

I'm happy that through this book you will learn that all is not lost, and even when you have outlasted your time on this Earth there's an eternal life awaiting you in heaven. God bless you.

Notes

ACKNOWLEDGMENTS

I would like to acknowledge my Bishop, Dr Sheldon Evans, and Dr Natalie Evans for being so instrumental in my journey to This is it. The prayers, prophetic utterances, the check-ins, the genuine concern, the love and respect you have displayed towards me, I am forever grateful.

To my EFLM leaders I want to acknowledge you for standing with me in the ministry when I needed all hands on deck. The intercessory prayers and your faithfulness, I honor and appreciate you all.

To my daughter Jaleen Goslin-Campbell who calls me every day to check up on me and to remind me how much she loves and appreciates me and the great future ahead of me. I love you first and always, my princess and to my grandson Navardinho Mason who has been my ride and live, I appreciate you.

www.ingramcontent.com/pod-product-compliance
Lightning Source LLC
Chambersburg PA
CBHW072203160426
43197CB00012B/2507